Viola
Scales, Arpeggios & Studies

for Trinity College London examinations from 2007

Initial–Grade 8

Published by
Trinity College London
Registered Office:
89 Albert Embankment
London SE1 7TP UK

T +44 (0)20 7820 6100
F +44 (0)20 7820 6161
E music@trinitycollege.co.uk
www.trinitycollege.co.uk

Registered in the UK
Company no. 02683033
Charity no. 1014792

Copyright © 2007 Trinity College London
Fifth impression, April 2014

Unauthorised photocopying is illegal
No part of this publication may be copied or reproduced in any
form or by any means without the prior permission of the publisher.

Printed in England by Halstan, Amersham, Bucks.

Examples of scale and arpeggio bowing patterns

The examples below are given as indications of bowing patterns for all instruments from the syllabus. Clefs, key and time signatures have been deliberately omitted in order not to imply an association with any one scale or member of the string family, or any particular interpretation or emphasis within each scale.

One octave scale, slurred in pairs

or

or (For Grade 1 only):

or

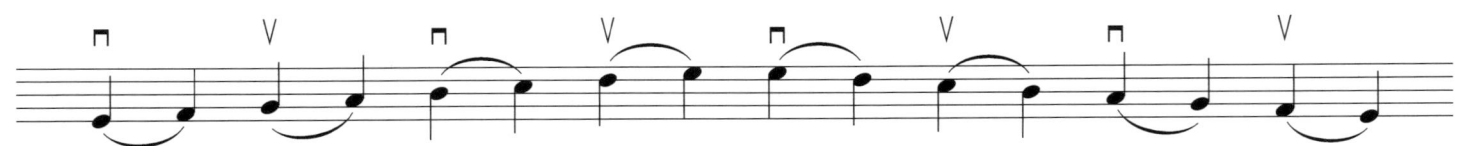

Two octave scale, slurred in pairs

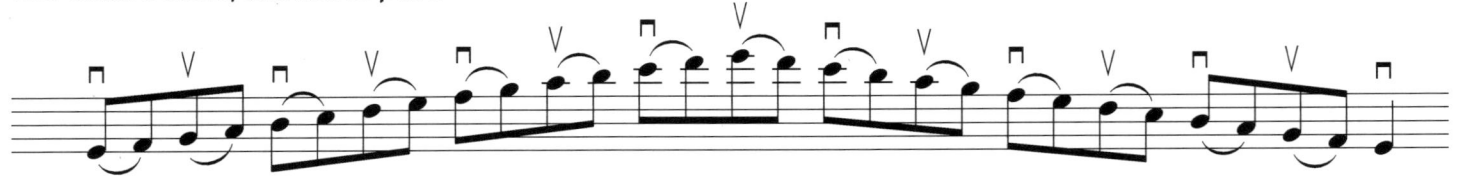

or

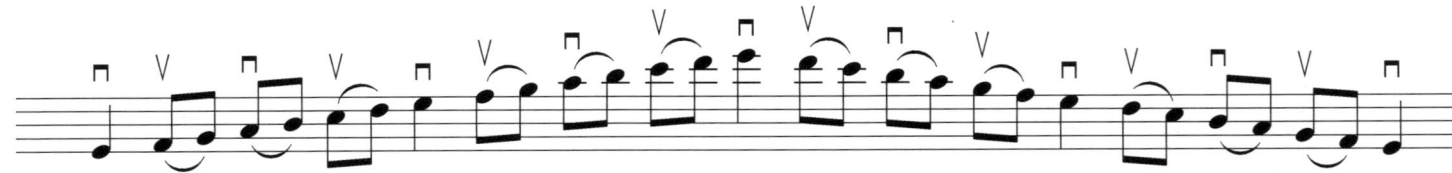

2

Scale slurred four notes to a bow

or

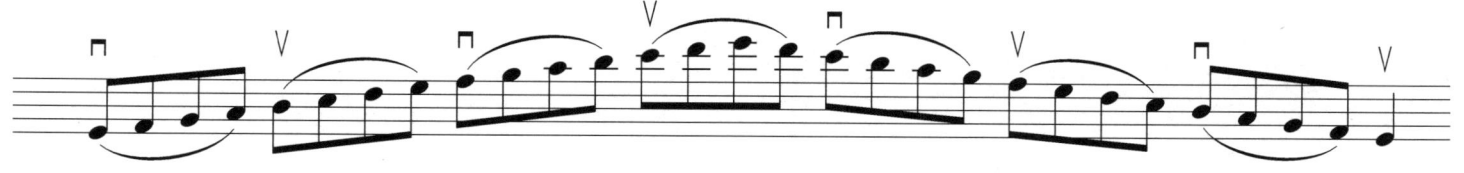

Scale slurred seven notes to a bow

or

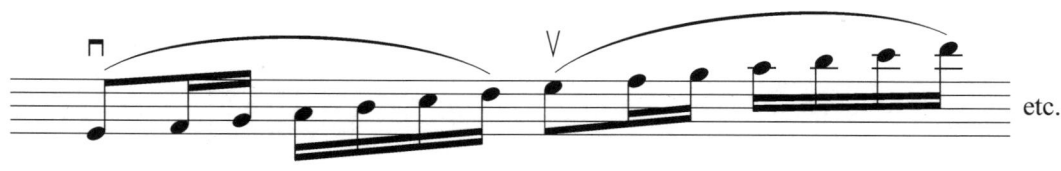

Scale slurred three notes to a bow

Arpeggio slurred in pairs

or

Arpeggio of a 7th slurred in pairs

Arpeggio slurred three notes to a bow (one octave)

Arpeggio slurred three notes to a bow (two octaves)

Arpeggio to a 12th slurred three notes to a bow

Initial

Scales (all from memory):

The following scales to be performed with the indicated rhythmic patterns on each note:

C major scale (one octave)

G major scale (one octave)

D major scale (one octave)

Grade 1

Candidate to prepare the Bowing Exercise and then *either* Section i) *or* Section ii) in full.

Bowing Exercise (from memory):

The candidate will be asked to play one scale of their own choice from any of those listed below for Grade 1.
The scale should be played with two separate crotchets on each degree of the scale, one down bow and one up bow.
For example:

Section i) Scales and Arpeggios (Group 1 *or* Group 2) & Technical Exercise (all from memory):

The candidate should prepare scales and arpeggios from **one** of the two groups listed below.
When the examiner requests a key, the candidate should play the scale and then, immediately (or after a moment's pause), the arpeggio.

Scales to be played with separate bows *and* slurred in pairs, as requested by the examiner.

Arpeggios to be played with separate bows only.

See pages 2-4 for rhythmic and bowing patterns.

Group 1:

F major scale (one octave, starting on the 3rd finger)

F major arpeggio (one octave, starting on the 3rd finger)

C major scale (one octave, starting on the 3rd finger)

C major arpeggio (one octave, starting on the 3rd finger)

G major scale (one octave, starting on the open string)

G major arpeggio (one octave, starting on the open string)

D major scale (one octave, starting on the open string)

D major arpeggio (one octave, starting on the open string)

G minor (to the 5th, starting on the open string, scale only)

or

Group 2:

C major scale (one octave, starting on the open string)

C major arpeggio (one octave, starting on the open string)

Grade 1 continued

G major scale (one octave, starting on the open string)

G major arpeggio (one octave, starting on the open string)

D major scale (one octave, starting from the 1st finger in 1st position)

D major arpeggio (one octave, starting from the 1st finger in 1st position)

A major scale (one octave, starting from the 1st finger in 1st position)

A major arpeggio (one octave, starting from the 1st finger in 1st position)

A minor (to the 5th, starting on the G string, scale only)

Technical Exercise (from memory):

Double Stops (open strings)

or Section ii) Studies:

Candidate to prepare the following three studies and to choose one of them to play first. The examiner will then select one of the remaining studies to be performed:

1. Floating Leaf in a Stream

2. Continental Song

Grade 1 continued

3. Marching On!

Grade 2

Candidate to prepare the Bowing Exercise and then *either* Section i) *or* Section ii) in full.

Bowing Exercise (from memory):

The candidate will be asked to play one scale of their own choice from any of those listed below for Grade 2. The scale should be played with the rhythm ♩ ♫ on each degree of the scale, separate bows.
For example:

(♩ = 80)

Section i) Scales and Arpeggios and Technical Exercise (all from memory):

The following scales and arpeggios to be prepared.
When the examiner requests a key, the candidate should play the scale and then, immediately (or after a moment's pause), the arpeggio.

Each scale/arpeggio pair to be played with separate bows *or* slurred in pairs, as requested by the examiner.

Minor scales to be played in *either* natural *or* harmonic *or* melodic form, at candidate's choice.

See pages 2-4 for rhythmic and bowing patterns.

C major scale (two octaves)

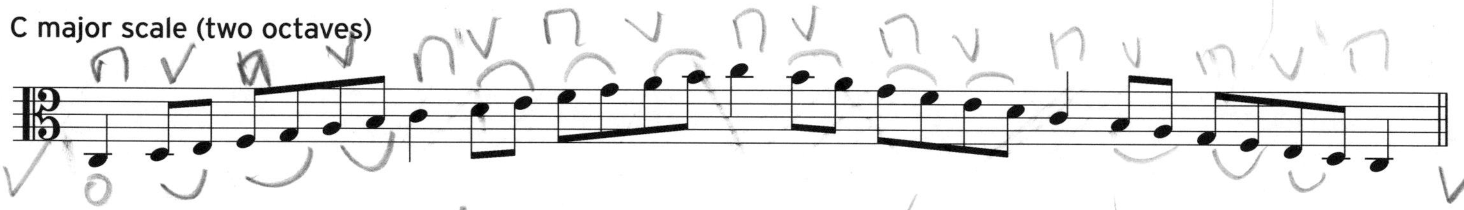

C major arpeggio (two octaves)

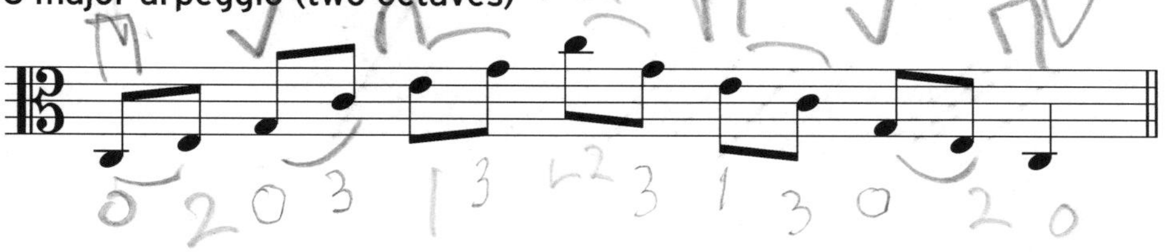

F major scale (one octave)

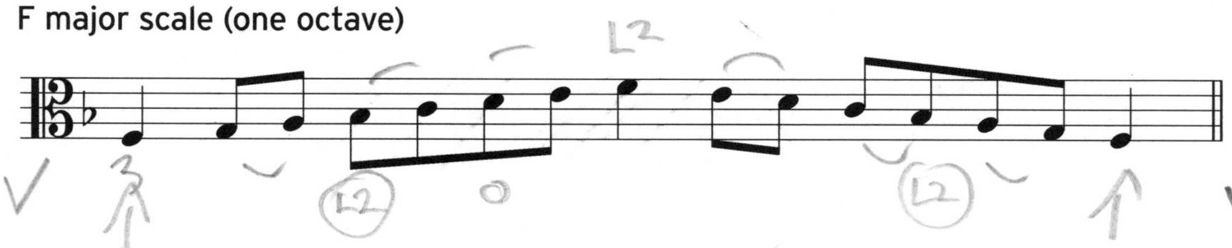

F major arpeggio (one octave)

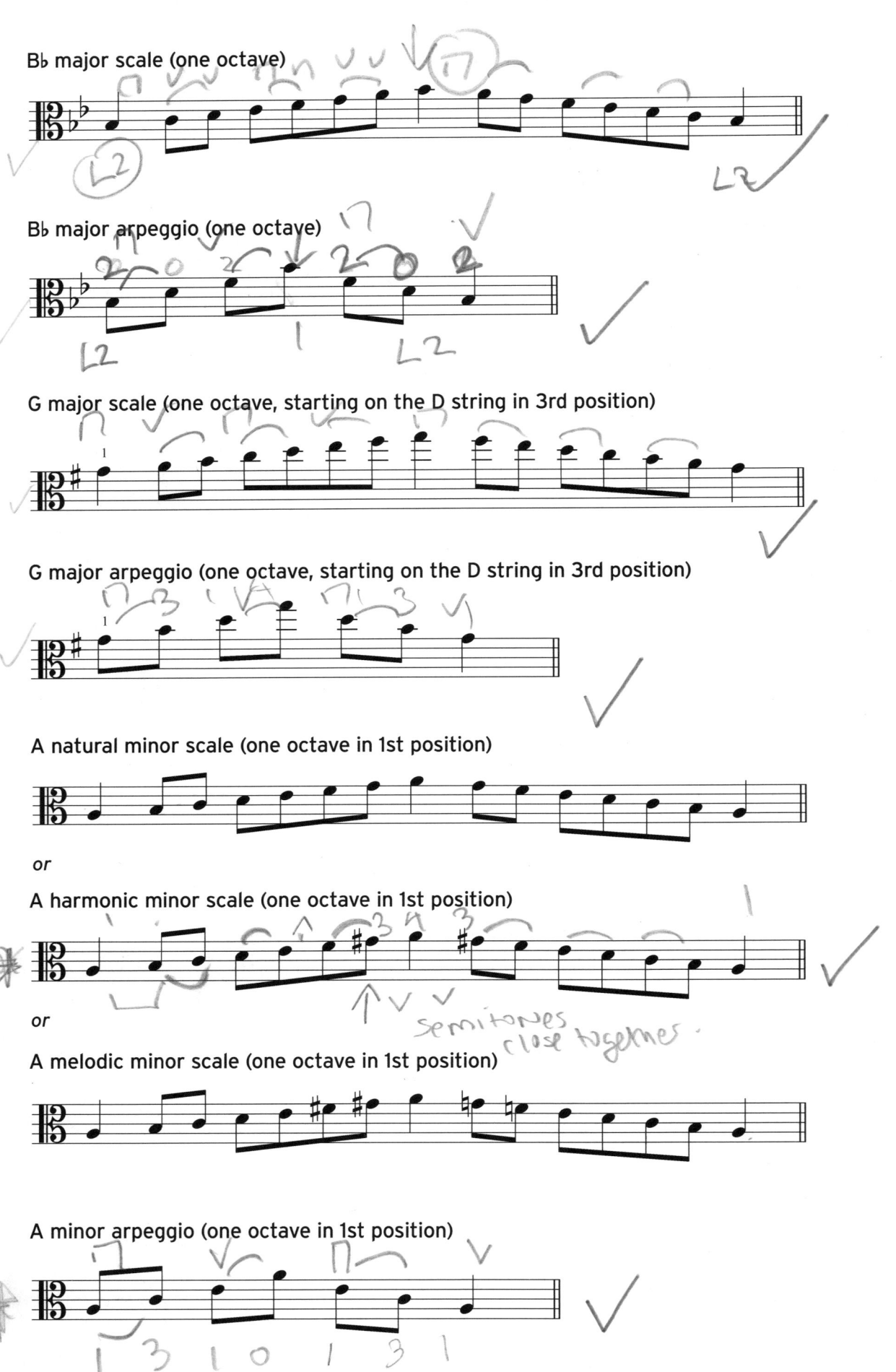

G natural minor scale (one octave in 1st position)

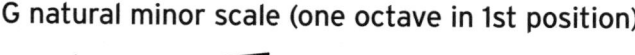

or

G harmonic minor scale (one octave in 1st position)

or

G melodic minor scale (one octave in 1st position)

G minor arpeggio (one octave in 1st position)

Technical Exercise (from memory):

Double Stops (octave and sixth)

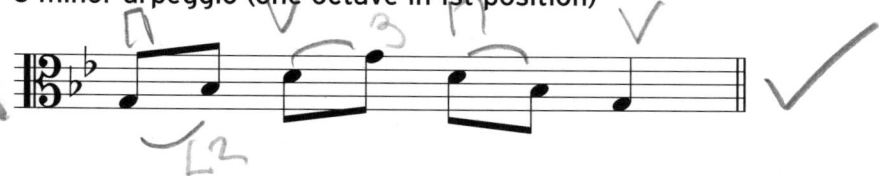

Grade 2 continued

or Section ii) Studies:

Candidate to prepare the following three studies and to choose one of them to play first. The examiner will then select one of the remaining studies to be performed:

1. Folk Dance

2. Farmer's Song

3. Royal Procession

Grade 3

Candidate to prepare the Bowing Exercise and then *either* Section i) *or* Section ii) in full:

Bowing Exercise (from memory):

The candidate will be asked to play one scale of their own choice from any of those listed below for Grade 3. The scale should be played with eight semiquavers on each degree of the scale, as in the following example given below in G major:

Section i) Scales and Arpeggios and Technical Exercises (all from memory):

The following scales and arpeggios to be prepared.

When the examiner requests a key, the candidate should play the scale and then, immediately (or after a moment's pause), the arpeggio.

Minor scales to be played in *either* harmonic *or* melodic form, at candidate's choice.

Scales to be prepared with separate bows *and* slurred in pairs.

Arpeggios to be prepared with separate bows *and* slurred three notes to a bow.

Dominant 7ths to be prepared with separate bows only.

See pages 2-4 for rhythmic and bowing patterns.

G major scale (two octaves, starting on the open string)

G major arpeggio (two octaves, starting on the open string)

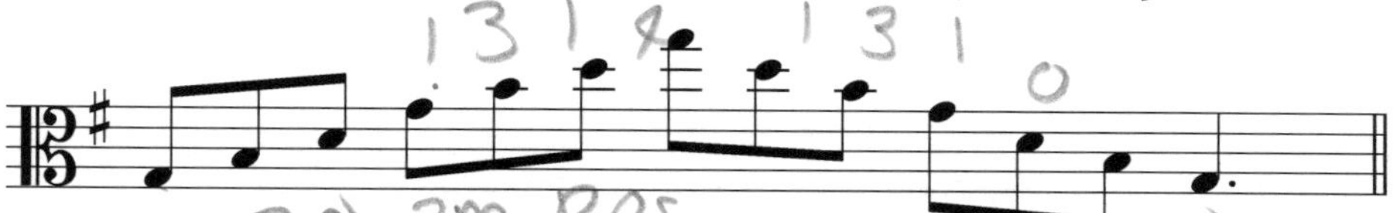

D major scale (two octaves)

D major arpeggio (two octaves)

Grade 3 continued

Bb major scale (one octave, starting on the G string in 2nd position)

Bb major arpeggio (one octave, starting on the G string in 2nd position)

Ab major scale (one octave)

Ab major arpeggio (one octave)

D harmonic minor scale (two octaves)

D melodic minor scale (two octaves)

D minor arpeggio (two octaves)

C harmonic minor scale (one octave starting on the G string)

or

C melodic minor scale (one octave starting on the G string)

C minor arpeggio (one octave starting on the G string)

Dominant 7th in the key of C (one octave, starting on G)

Dominant 7th in the key of D (one octave, starting on A)

Technical Exercises (from memory):

The following exercises to be performed in the patterns shown:

a) Chromatic Phrase:

to be performed with separate bows, starting on the G string:

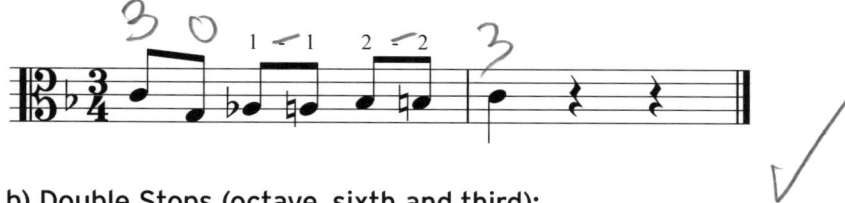

b) Double Stops (octave, sixth and third):

Grade 3 continued

or Section ii) Studies:

Candidate to prepare the following three studies and to choose one of them to play first. The examiner will then select one of the remaining studies to be performed:

1. Sweet and Sour Waltz

2. Space Journey

3. Fond Memories

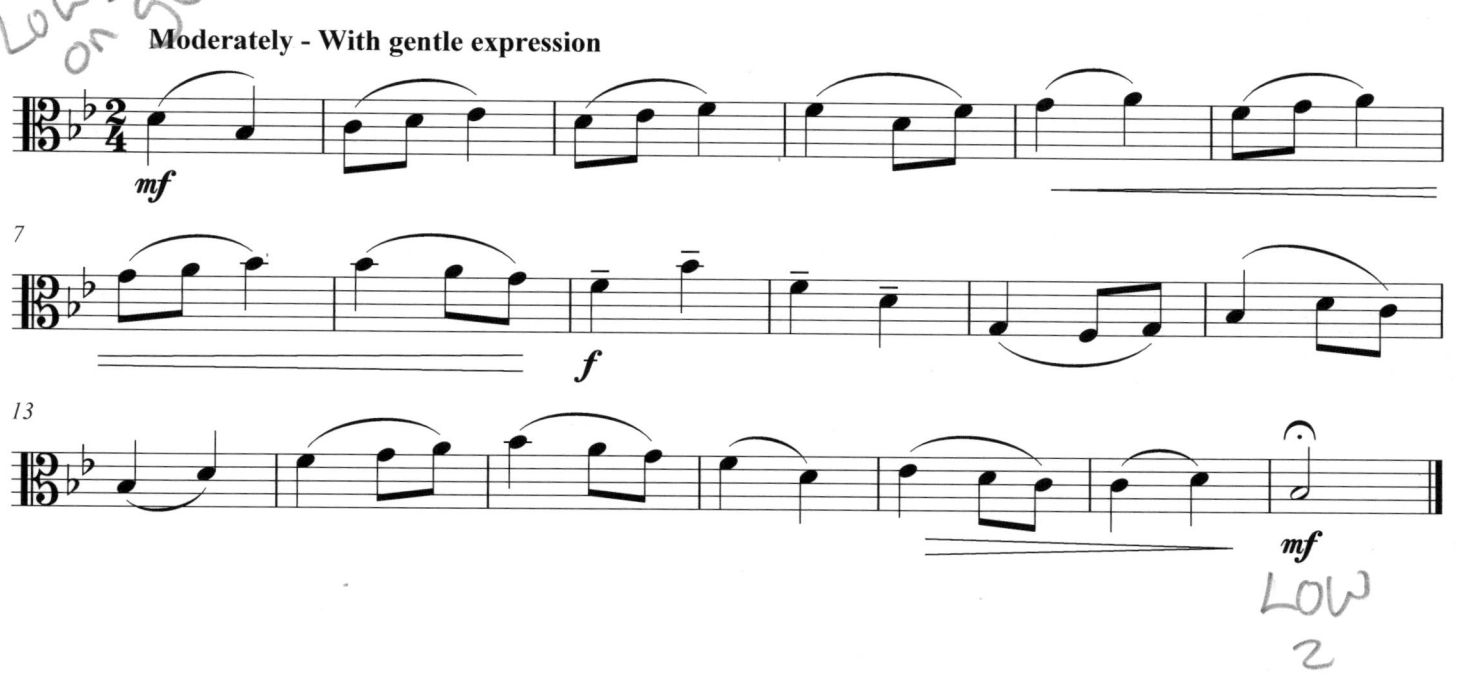

Grade 4

Candidate to prepare the Bowing Exercise and then *either* Section i) *or* Section ii) in full.

Bowing Exercise (from memory):

The candidate will be asked to play one scale of their own choice from any of those listed below for Grade 4. The scale should be played with the rhythm ♩. ♪♩ on each degree of the scale, as in the following example given below in F major:

($\dotted{h}$ = 50)

Section i) Scales and Arpeggios and Technical Exercises (all from memory):

The following scales and arpeggios to be prepared.

When the examiner requests a key, the candidate should play the scale and then, immediately (or after a moment's pause), the arpeggio.

Minor scales to be played in *either* harmonic *or* melodic form, at candidate's choice.

Scales to be prepared with separate bows *and* slurred four notes to a bow.

Arpeggios to be prepared with separate bows *and* slurred three notes to a bow.

Dominant 7ths to be prepared with separate bows *and* slurred four notes to a bow.

Chromatic scale to be prepared with separate bows only.

See pages 2-4 for rhythmic and bowing patterns.

F major scale (two octaves)

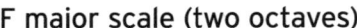

F major arpeggio (two octaves)

E♭ major scale (two octaves)

E♭ major arpeggio (two octaves)

A major scale (one octave, starting on the D string in 4th position)

A major arpeggio (one octave, starting on the D string in 4th position)

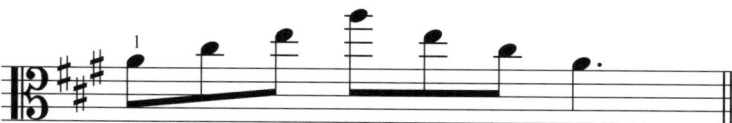

F harmonic minor scale (two octaves)

or

F melodic minor scale (two octaves)

F minor arpeggio (two octaves)

E♭ harmonic minor scale (two octaves)

or

E♭ melodic minor scale (two octaves)

E♭ minor arpeggio (two octaves)

Grade 4 continued

A harmonic minor scale (one octave, starting on the D string in 4th position)

or

A melodic minor scale (one octave, starting on the D string in 4th position)

A minor arpeggio (one octave, starting on the D string in 4th position)

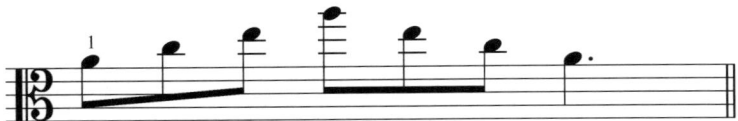

Dominant 7th in the key of F (one octave, starting on C)

Dominant 7th in the key of G (one octave, starting on D)

Dominant 7th in the key of A♭ (one octave, starting on E♭)

Chromatic scale starting on G (one octave)

Technical Exercises (from memory):

a) Octaves:

b) G major phrase:

or Section ii) Studies:

Candidate to prepare the following three studies and to choose one of them to play first. The examiner will then select one of the remaining studies to be performed:

1. Hungarian Violas!

Grade 4 continued

2. The Grand House

3. Rustic Dance

Grade 5

Candidate to prepare the Bowing Exercise and then *either* Section i) *or* Section ii) in full.

Bowing Exercise (from memory):

The candidate will be asked to play one scale of their own choice from any of those listed below for Grade 5. The scale should be played with a martelé* bow stroke. (♩ = 88)

Section i) Scales and Arpeggios and Technical Exercises (all from memory):

The following scales and arpeggios to be prepared.

When the examiner requests a key, the candidate should play the scale and then, immediately (or after a moment's pause), the arpeggio.

Minor scales to be played in *either* melodic *or* harmonic form, at candidate's choice.

3-octave scales and arpeggios to be prepared with separate bows *and* slurred three notes to a bow.

2-octave scales and arpeggios to be prepared with separate bows *and* slurred four notes to a bow (scales) *and* six notes to a bow (arpeggios).

Dominant 7ths to be prepared with separate bows *and* slurred four notes to a bow.

Chromatic scales to be prepared with separate bows *and* slurred four notes to a bow.

Diminished 7th to be prepared with separate bows only.

See pages 2–4 for rhythmic and bowing patterns.

C major scale (three octaves)

C major arpeggio (three octaves)

E major scale (two octaves)

*__Martelé:__ Immediately after the initial 'bite' or pressure accent the pressure must be released. The bow moves quickly but does not leave the string. Each stroke should end before applying pressure for the 'bite' at the start of the new stroke. This will result in an inevitable small silence between each note.

Grade 5 continued

E major arpeggio (two octaves)

A major scale (two octaves)

A major arpeggio (two octaves)

D♭ major scale (two octaves)

D♭ major arpeggio (two octaves)

C harmonic minor scale (three octaves)

or

C melodic minor scale (three octaves)

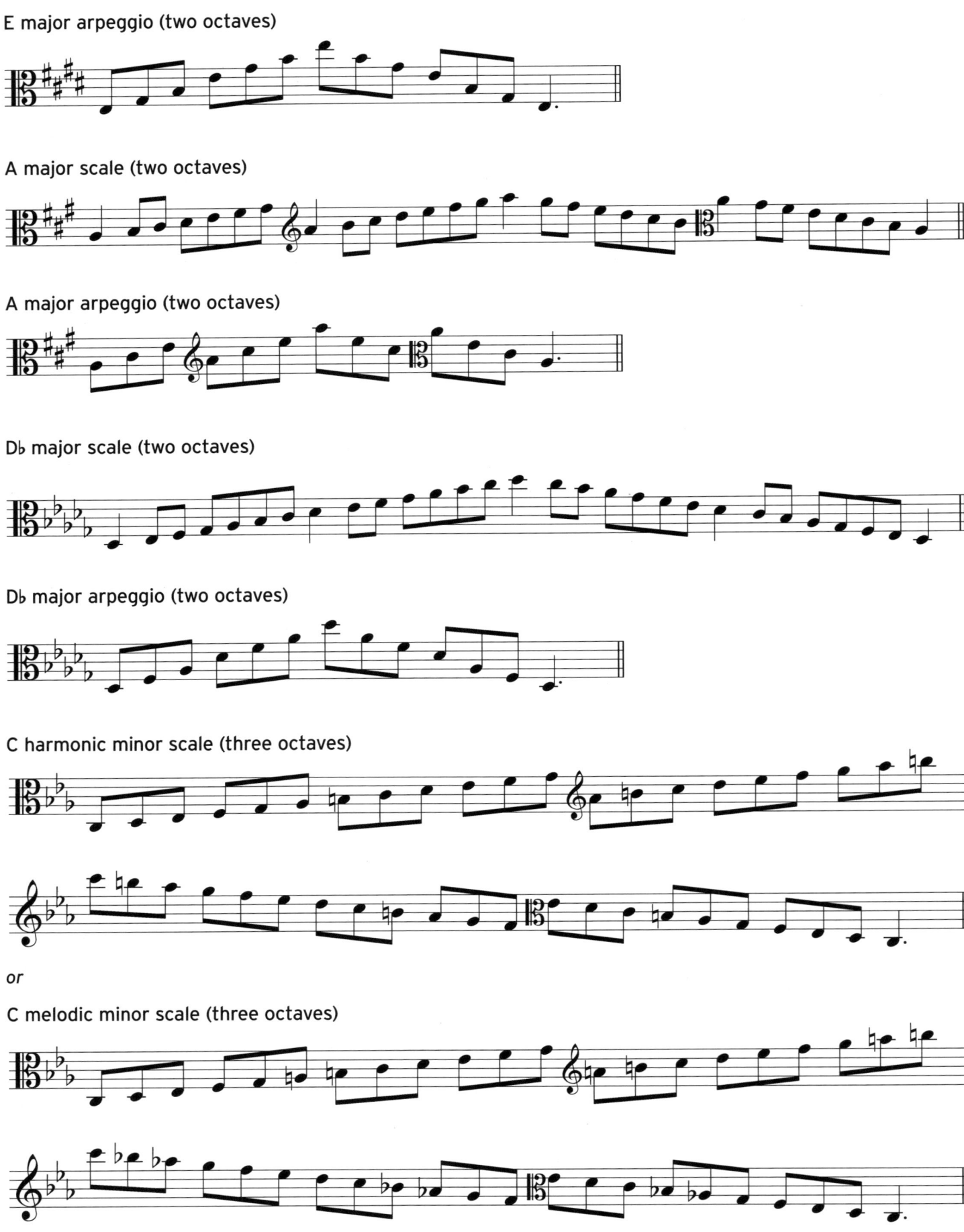

C minor arpeggio (three octaves)

E harmonic minor scale (two octaves)

or

E melodic minor scale (two octaves)

E minor arpeggio (two octaves)

A harmonic minor scale (two octaves)

or

A melodic minor scale (two octaves)

A minor arpeggio (two octaves)

Grade 5 continued

C# harmonic minor scale (two octaves)

or

C# melodic minor scale (two octaves)

C# minor arpeggio (two octaves)

Dominant 7th in the key of F (two octaves, starting on C)

Dominant 7th in the key of G♭ (two octaves, starting on D♭)

Chromatic scale starting on C (two octaves)

Chromatic scale starting on D (two octaves)

Diminished 7th starting on G (one octave)

Technical Exercises (from memory):

a) F major in double-stopped thirds:

b) E♭ major in double-stopped sixths:

c) G major scale on one string:

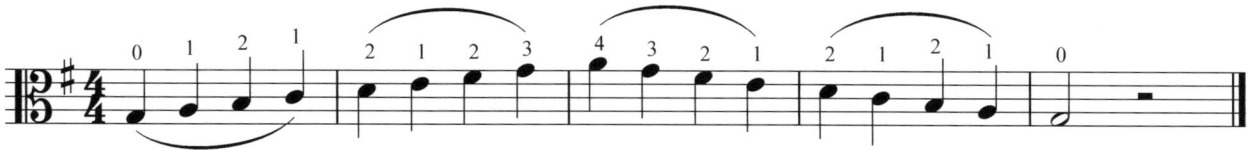

Grade 5 continued

or Section ii) Studies:

Candidate to prepare the following three studies and to choose one of them to play first. The examiner will then select one of the remaining studies to be performed:

1. Country Fair

2. Bee-Bop Blues

Grade 5 continued

3. Heroic Film Tune

Grade 6

Candidate to prepare the Bowing Exercise and then *either* Section i) *or* Section ii) in full.

Bowing Exercise (from memory):

The candidate will be asked to play one scale of their own choice from any of those listed below for Grade 6. Each note of the scale should be played as two spiccato* quavers. (♩ = 150)

Section i) Scales and Arpeggios and Technical Exercises (all from memory):

The candidate should prepare major and minor scales and arpeggios from Group 1 *or* Group 2. Additionally, **all** candidates should prepare the chromatic scale, diminished 7th arpeggio and technical exercises listed on pages 38-39.

When the examiner requests a major tonal centre, the candidate should play in succession:
    The major scale
    The major arpeggio
    The dominant 7th starting on that note and resolving onto the tonic

When the examiner requests a minor tonal centre, the candidate should play in succession:
    The melodic minor scale
    The harmonic minor scale
    The minor arpeggio

The candidate may pause briefly between individual scales and arpeggios.

3-octave scales and arpeggios to be prepared with separate bows *and* slurred three notes to a bow.

2-octave scales and arpeggios to be prepared with separate bows *and* slurred four notes to a bow (scales) *and* six notes to a bow (arpeggios).

Dominant 7ths to be prepared with separate bows *and* slurred four notes to a bow.

Diminished 7th to be prepared with separate bows *and* slurred four notes to a bow.

Chromatic scale to be prepared with separate bows *and* slurred four notes to a bow.

See pages 2-4 for rhythmic and bowing patterns.

Group 1 — D, B♭, A♭/G♯ tonal centres:

D major scale (three octaves)

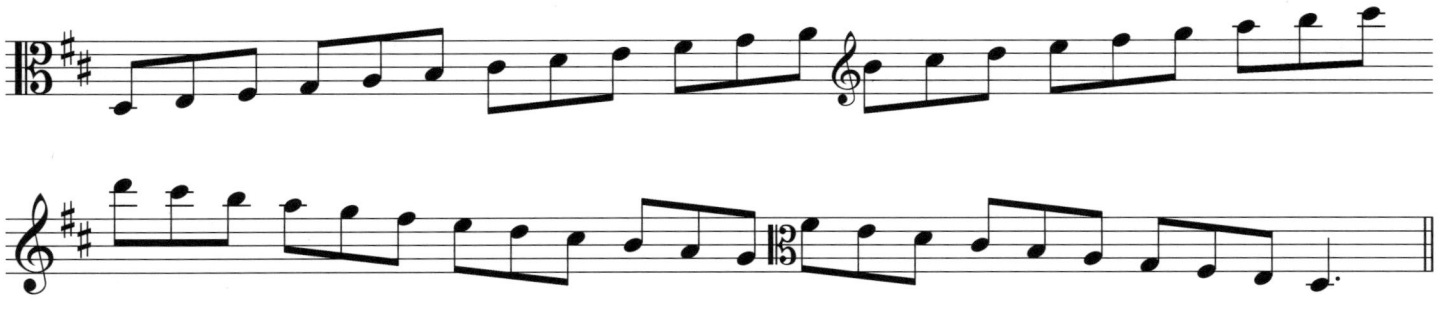

D major arpeggio (three octaves)

*****Spiccato:** the bow starts off the string and leaves the string after every note, creating a small 'saucer' or 'smile' shape over the string, touching the string at the lowest point of the 'saucer' or 'smile' shape.

Grade 6 continued

Dominant 7th in the key of G, starting on D (three octaves)

D melodic minor scale (three octaves)

D harmonic minor scale (three octaves)

D minor arpeggio (three octaves)

B♭ major scale (two octaves)

B♭ major arpeggio (two octaves)

Dominant 7th in the key of E♭, starting on B♭ (two octaves)

B♭ melodic minor scale (two octaves)

B♭ harmonic minor scale (two octaves)

B♭ minor arpeggio (two octaves)

A♭ major scale (two octaves)

A♭ major arpeggio (two octaves)

Dominant 7th in the key of D♭, starting on A♭ (two octaves)

G♯ melodic minor scale (two octaves)

Grade 6 continued

G# harmonic minor scale (two octaves)

G# minor arpeggio (two octaves)

or

Group 2 – D, B, F# tonal centres:

D tonal centre (see pages 33-34)

B major scale (two octaves)

B major arpeggio (two octaves)

Dominant 7th in the key of E, starting on B (two octaves)

B melodic minor scale (two octaves)

B harmonic minor scale (two octaves)

B minor arpeggio (two octaves)

F# major scale (two octaves)

F# major arpeggio (two octaves)

Dominant 7th in the key of B, starting on F# (two octaves)

F# melodic minor scale (two octaves)

F# harmonic minor scale (two octaves)

F# minor arpeggio (two octaves)

Grade 6 continued

All candidates should prepare the following:

Chromatic scale starting on E♭ (two octaves)

Diminished 7th starting on C (two octaves)

Technical Exercises (from memory):

a) G major in double-stopped thirds:

b) A♭ major in double-stopped sixths:

c) G major in double-stopped octaves:

d) A major scale on one string:

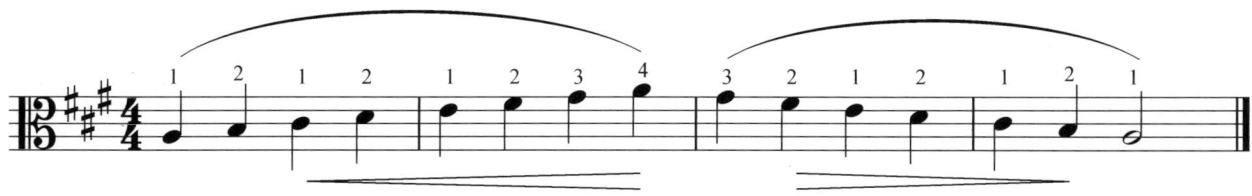

or Section ii) Orchestral Excerpts. See Strings syllabus for details.

Grade 7

Candidate to prepare the Bowing Exercise and then *either* Section i) *or* Section ii) in full.

Bowing Exercise (from memory):

The candidate will be asked to play one scale of their own choice from any of those listed below for Grade 7. The whole scale should be played with hooked* bowing, as in the following example (♩ = 120):

Section i) Scales and Arpeggios and Technical Exercises (all from memory):

The candidate should prepare major and minor scales and arpeggios from Group 1 *or* Group 2. Additionally, **all** candidates should prepare chromatic scales, diminished 7th arpeggios and technical exercises listed on pages 48-49.

When the examiner requests a major tonal centre, the candidate should play in succession:
   The major scale
   The major arpeggio
   The dominant 7th starting on that note and resolving onto the tonic

When the examiner requests a minor tonal centre, the candidate should play in succession:
   The melodic minor scale
   The harmonic minor scale
   The minor arpeggio

The candidate may pause briefly between individual scales and arpeggios.

All scales to be prepared with separate bows *and* slurred seven notes to a bow.

All arpeggios to be prepared with separate bows *and* slurred nine notes to a bow.

Dominant 7ths to be prepared with separate bows *and* slurred four notes to a bow.

Chromatic scales to be prepared with separate bows *and* slurred six notes to a bow.

Diminished 7ths to be prepared with separate bows *and* slurred four notes to a bow.

See pages 2-4 for rhythmic and bowing patterns.

Group 1 – C, E, D♭/C♯ tonal centres:

C major scale (three octaves)

*Hooked bowing: this describes a method of bowing a repeated dotted quaver-semiquaver rhythm.

C major arpeggio (three octaves)

Dominant 7th in the key of F, starting on C (three octaves)

C melodic minor scale (three octaves)

C harmonic minor scale (three octaves)

C minor arpeggio (three octaves)

Grade 7 continued

E major scale (three octaves)

E major arpeggio (three octaves)

Dominant 7th in the key of A, starting on E (three octaves)

E melodic minor scale (three octaves)

E harmonic minor scale (three octaves)

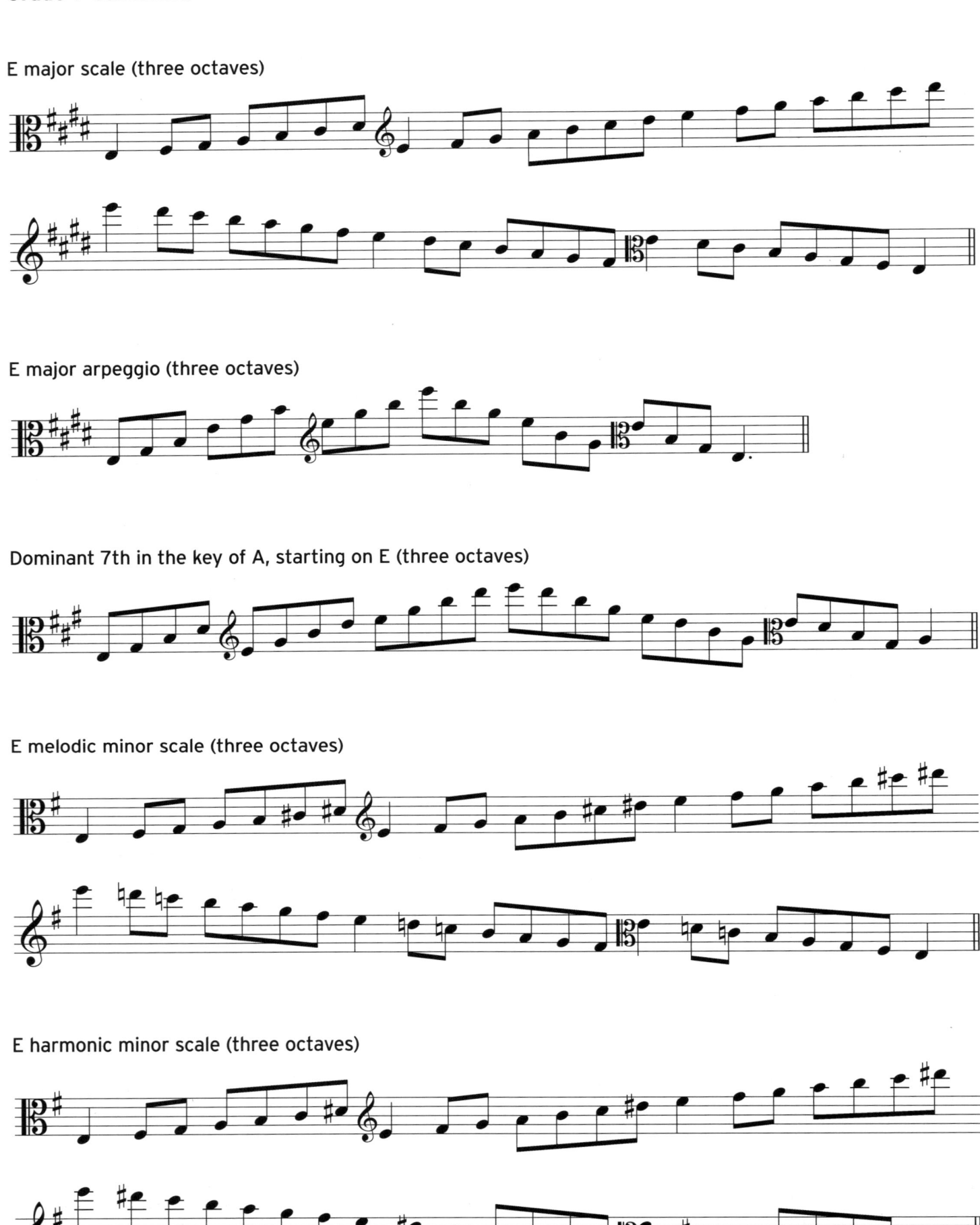

E minor arpeggio (three octaves)

Db major scale (three octaves)

Db major arpeggio (three octaves)

Dominant 7th in the key of Gb, starting on Db (three octaves)

C# melodic minor scale (three octaves)

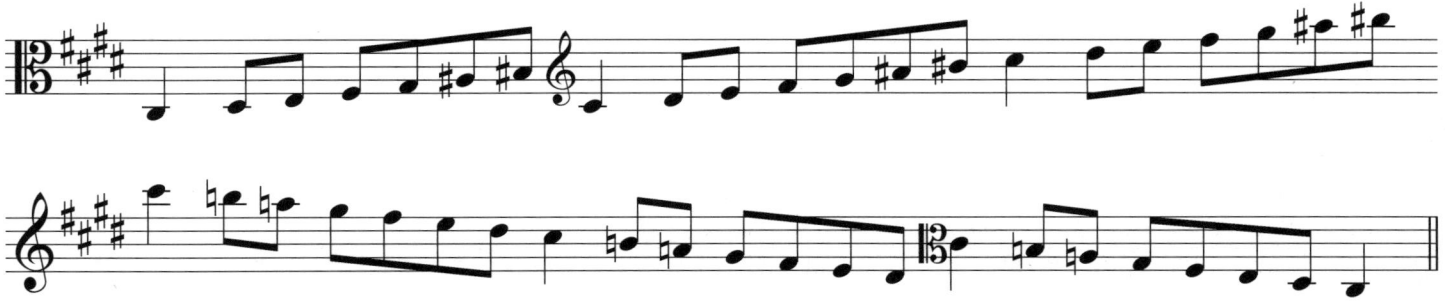

Grade 7 continued

C# harmonic minor scale (three octaves)

C# minor arpeggio (three octaves)

or

Group 2 – G, D, E tonal centres:

G major scale (three octaves)

G major arpeggio (three octaves)

Dominant 7th in the key of C, starting on G (three octaves)

G melodic minor scale (three octaves)

G harmonic minor scale (three octaves)

G minor arpeggio (three octaves)

D major scale (three octaves)

D major arpeggio (three octaves)

Grade 7 continued

Dominant 7th in the key of G, starting on D (three octaves)

D melodic minor scale (three octaves)

D harmonic minor scale (three octaves)

D minor arpeggio (three octaves)

E major scale (three octaves)

E major arpeggio (three octaves)

Dominant 7th in the key of A, starting on E (three octaves)

E melodic minor scale (three octaves)

E harmonic minor scale (three octaves)

E minor arpeggio (three octaves)

Grade 7 continued

All candidates should prepare the following:

Chromatic scale starting on E (two octaves)

Chromatic scale starting on D♭ (two octaves)

Diminished 7th starting on D (two octaves)

Diminished 7th starting on C♯/D♭ (two octaves)

Technical Exercises (from memory):

Double Stops

a) F major in thirds (one octave):

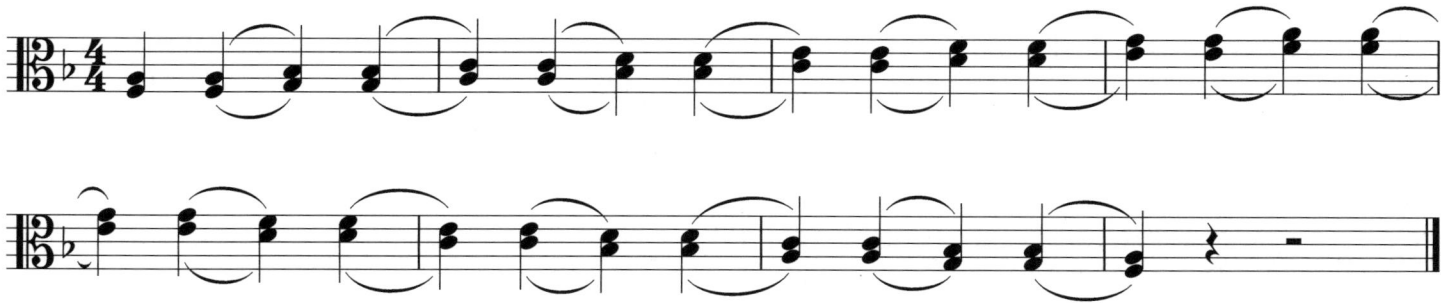

b) G major in thirds (one octave):

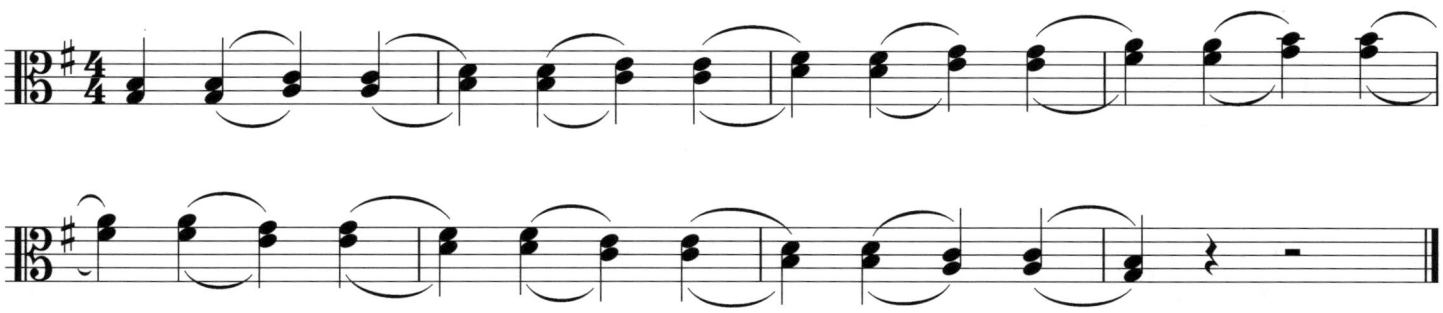

c) E♭ major in sixths (one octave):

d) G major in octaves (one octave):

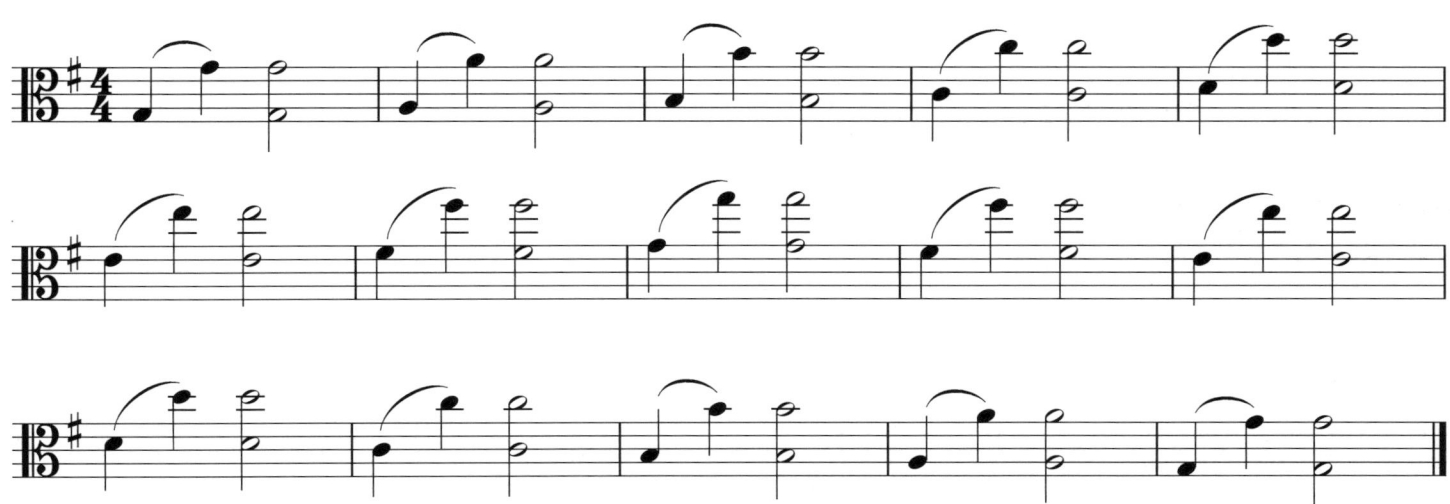

or Section ii) Orchestral Excerpts. See Strings syllabus for details.

Grade 8

Candidate to prepare the Bowing Exercise and then *either* Section i) *or* Section ii) in full.

Bowing Exercise (from memory):

The candidate will be asked to play one scale of their own choice from any of those listed below for Grade 8. The examiner will choose any **one** of the specified bowings from previous grades and ask the candidate to play their scale with that bowing.

Section i) Scales and Arpeggios and Technical Exercises (all from memory):

The candidate should prepare major and minor scales and arpeggios from Group 1 *or* Group 2. Additionally, candidates should prepare chromatic scales and diminished 7th arpeggios from their chosen groups, and technical exercises, listed on pages 60-64.

When the examiner requests a major tonal centre, the candidate should play in succession:
    The major scale
    The major arpeggio
    The dominant 7th starting on that note and resolving onto the tonic

When the examiner requests a minor tonal centre, the candidate should play in succession:
    The melodic minor scale
    The harmonic minor scale
    The minor arpeggio

The candidate may pause briefly between individual scales and arpeggios.

All scales and arpeggios to be prepared with separate bows *and* slurred one bow ascending, one bow descending and a separate bow for the last note.

Dominant 7ths to be prepared with separate bows *and* slurred four notes to a bow.

Chromatic scales (starting on each of the four notes of the chosen group) to be prepared with separate bows *and* slurred twelve notes to a bow.

Diminished 7ths (starting on each of the four notes of the chosen group) to be prepared with separate bows *and* slurred eight notes to a bow.

See pages 2-4 for rhythmic and bowing patterns.

Group 1 – C, D, A♭/G♯, F♯ tonal centres:

C major scale (three octaves)

C major arpeggio (three octaves)

Dominant 7th in the key of F, starting on C (three octaves)

C melodic minor scale (three octaves)

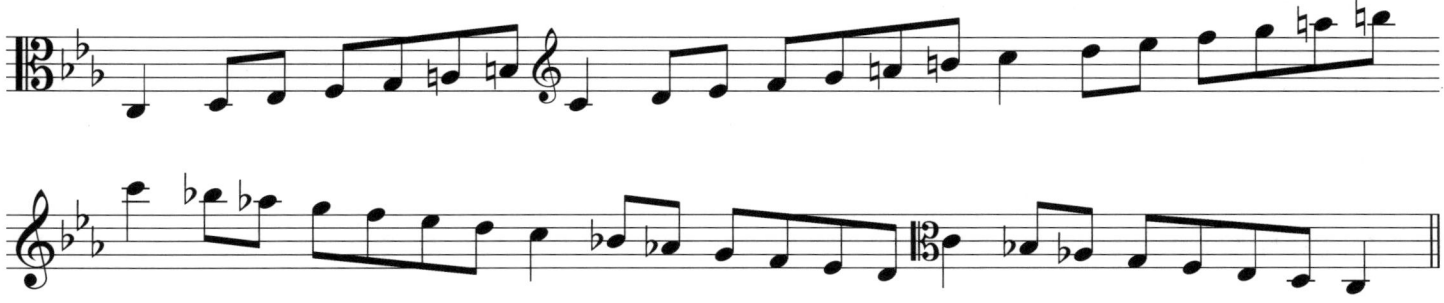

C harmonic minor scale (three octaves)

C minor arpeggio (three octaves)

D major scale (three octaves)

Grade 8 continued

D major arpeggio (three octaves)

Dominant 7th in the key of G, starting on D (three octaves)

D melodic minor scale (three octaves)

D harmonic minor scale (three octaves)

D minor arpeggio (three octaves)

A♭ major scale (three octaves)

A♭ major arpeggio (three octaves)

Dominant 7th in the key of D♭, starting on A♭ (three octaves)

G# melodic minor scale (three octaves)

G# harmonic minor scale (three octaves)

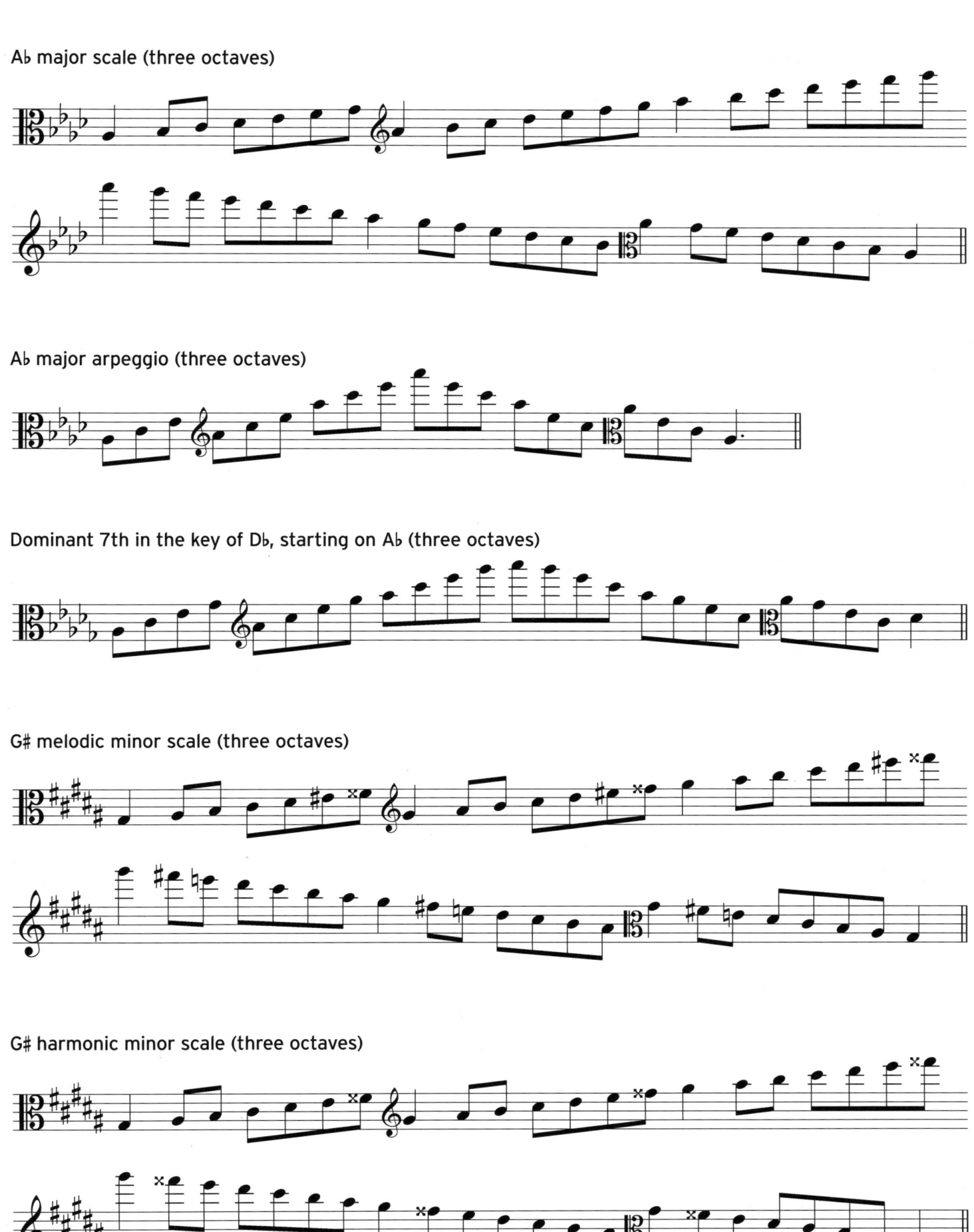

Grade 8 continued

G# minor arpeggio (three octaves)

F# major scale (three octaves)

F# major arpeggio (three octaves)

Dominant 7th in the key of B, starting on F# (three octaves)

F# melodic minor scale (three octaves)

F# harmonic minor scale (three octaves)

F# minor arpeggio (three octaves)

or

Group 2 – F, G, E♭, D♭/C# tonal centres:

F major scale (three octaves)

F major arpeggio (three octaves)

Dominant 7th in the key of B♭, starting on F (three octaves)

Grade 8 continued

F melodic minor scale (three octaves)

F harmonic minor scale (three octaves)

F minor arpeggio (three octaves)

G major scale (three octaves)

G major arpeggio (three octaves)

Dominant 7th in the key of C, starting on G (three octaves)

G melodic minor scale (three octaves)

G harmonic minor scale (three octaves)

G minor arpeggio (three octaves)

E♭ major scale (three octaves)

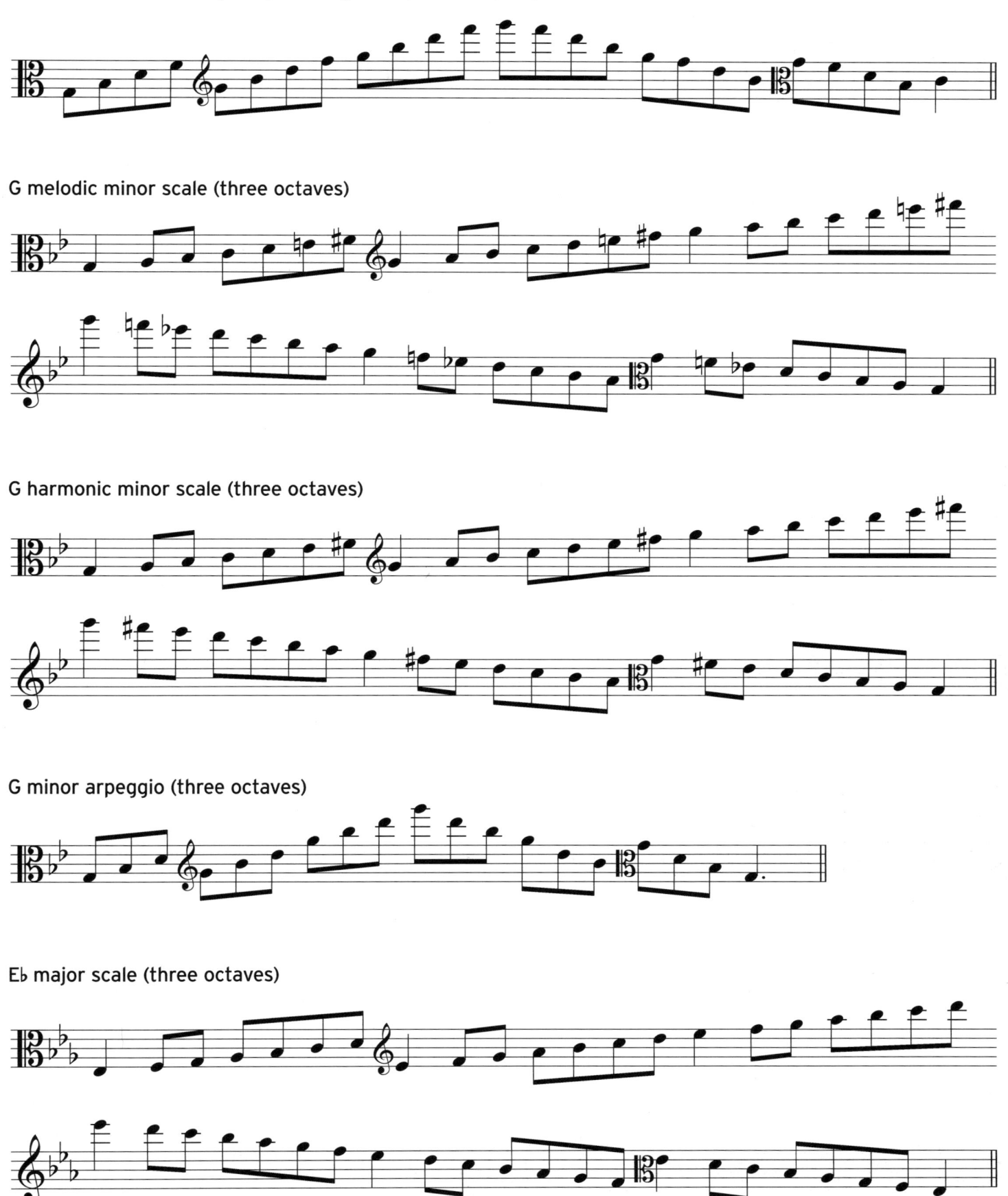

Grade 8 continued

Eb major arpeggio (three octaves)

Dominant 7th in the key of Ab, starting on Eb (three octaves)

Eb melodic minor scale (three octaves)

Eb harmonic minor scale (three octaves)

Eb minor arpeggio (three octaves)

Db major scale (three octaves)

Db major arpeggio (three octaves)

Dominant 7th in the key of Gb, starting on Db (three octaves)

C# melodic minor scale (three octaves)

C# harmonic minor scale (three octaves)

C# minor arpeggio (three octaves)

Grade 8 continued

Group 1 Chromatic Scales:

Chromatic scale starting on C (two octaves)

Chromatic scale starting on D (two octaves)

Chromatic scale starting on A♭ (two octaves)

Chromatic scale starting on F♯ (two octaves)

or

Group 2 Chromatic Scales:

Chromatic scale starting on F (two octaves)

Chromatic scale starting on G (two octaves)

Chromatic scale starting on E♭ (two octaves)

Chromatic scale starting on D♭ (two octaves)

Grade 8 continued

Group 1 Diminished 7ths:

Diminished 7th starting on C (two octaves)

Diminished 7th starting on D (two octaves)

Diminished 7th starting on G#/A♭ (two octaves)

Diminished 7th starting on F#/G♭ (two octaves)

or

Group 2 Diminished 7ths:

Diminished 7th starting on F (two octaves)

Diminished 7th starting on G (two octaves)

Diminished 7th starting on D♯/E♭ (two octaves)

Diminished 7th starting on C♯/D♭ (two octaves)

Technical Exercises (from memory):

a) F major in thirds (two octaves):

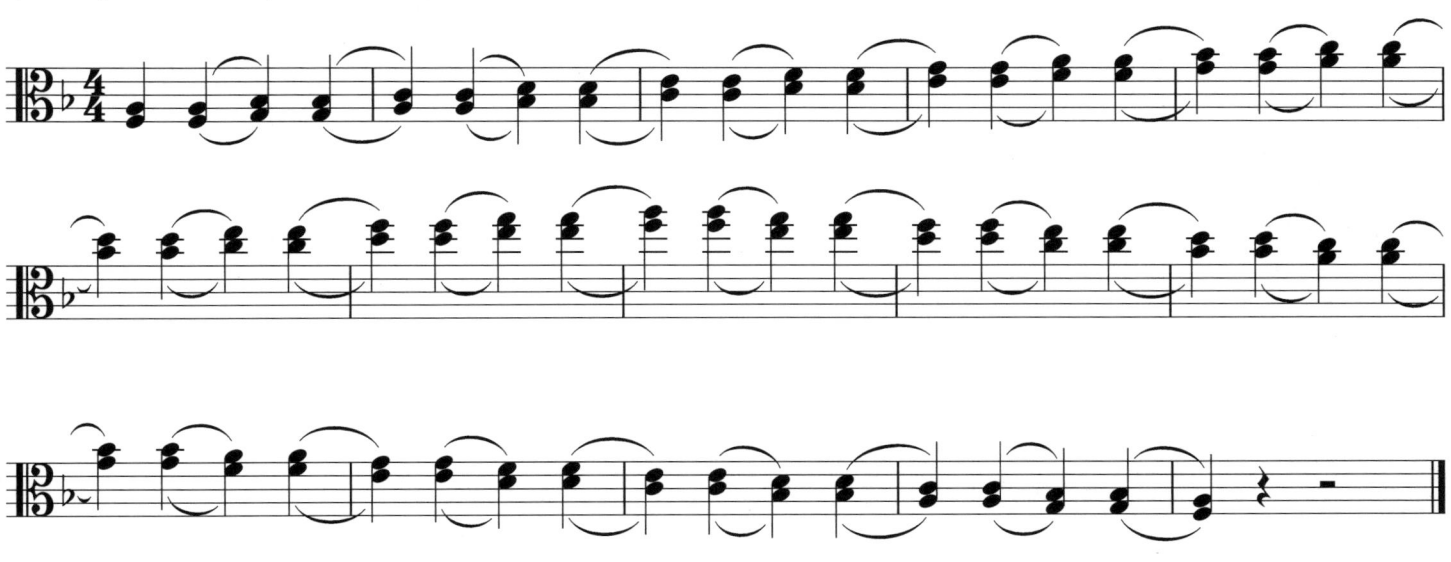

b) G major in thirds (two octaves):

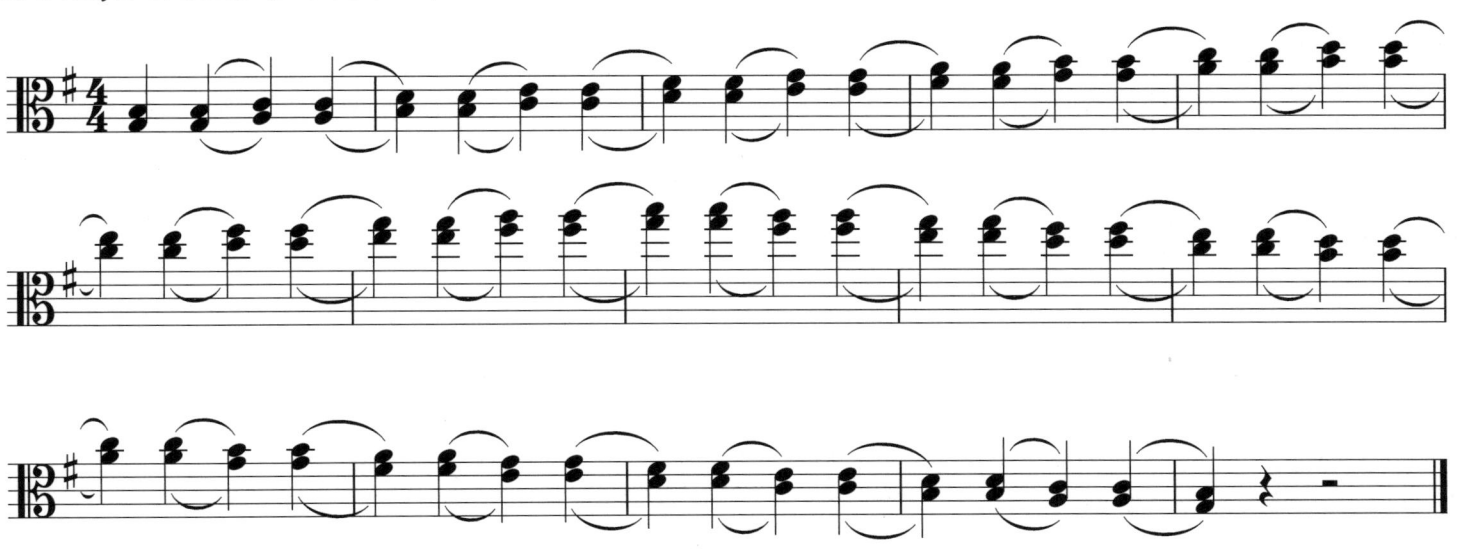

Grade 8 continued

c) C major in sixths (two octaves):

d) C major in octaves (two octaves):

or Section ii) Orchestral Excerpts. See Strings syllabus for details.